21st Century Skills Library

ANIMAL INVADERS

WALKING CATFISH

Susan H. Gray

Cherry Lake Publishing
Ann Arbor, Michigan

Published in the United States of America by Cherry Lake Publishing
Ann Arbor, MI
www.cherrylakepublishing.com

Content Adviser: John P. Sullivan, PhD, Department of Ichthyology, The Academy of
Natural Sciences, Philadelphia, Pennsylvania

Please note: Our map is as up-to-date as possible at the time of publication.

Photo Credits: Cover and pages 1, 10, and 14, ©BRUCE COLEMAN INC./Alamy; pages
4, 6, 8, 16, and 24, ©Paul Shafland, Courtesy of Florida Fish and Wildlife Conservation
Commission (FWC); page 12, ©Bob Gibbons/Alamy; page 19, ©Asther Lau Choon Siew,
used under license from Shutterstock, Inc.; page 20, ©Sally Scott, used under license
from Shutterstock, Inc.; page 26, ©blickwinkel/alamy

Map by XNR Productions Inc.

Library of Congress Cataloging-in-Publication Data
Gray, Susan Heinrichs.
 Walking catfish / by Susan H. Gray.
    p. cm.—(Animal invaders)
 Includes index.
 ISBN-13: 978-1-60279-242-5
 ISBN-10: 1-60279-242-9
 1. Walking catfish—Juvenile literature. I. Title. II. Series.
 QL638.C6G73 2009
 597'.49—dc22   2008000804

*Cherry Lake Publishing would like to acknowledge the work of
The Partnership for 21st Century Skills.
Please visit www.21stcenturyskills.org for more information.*

TABLE OF CONTENTS

CHAPTER ONE

OUT FOR A WALK

*A walking catfish comes out of the water in
search of a pond with more food.*

A catfish is exploring the bottom of a pond. Its long,
fleshy feelers slowly glide over the smooth rocks and gently
tap the gravel. The feelers have special sensors that taste
everything they touch.

The pond offers very little food, and the fish senses that it should go elsewhere. It flares out the fins and spines behind its head. Then the spines bend downward, pressing into the gravel. Flexing its body back and forth, the catfish "walks" on its spines. The catfish makes its way to the pond's edge. Then up the bank it goes. It thrashes back and forth and gulps for air.

It's a strange sight. But it's not unusual for the walking catfish (*Clarias batrachus*). This catfish needs a better home—one with plenty of food. And walking is the only way to get there.

Quite often, people who travel to other parts of the world bring unfamiliar types, or **species**, of plants and animals back home with them. Some plan to keep the animals as pets. Some hope to grow the plants in their backyards. And some want to raise the plants or animals on farms.

If these plants and animals have no enemies in their new homes, they can grow out of control. They might completely take over an area. A new type of plant or animal that moves into a country and becomes a problem is called an invasive species.

Centuries ago, invasive species were not a great problem. But today, there are hundreds of invasive species in countries all over the world. How are things different today? Why are there so many invasive species?

CHAPTER TWO

AN UNUSUAL LIFE

Walking catfish are usually gray in color, but they
can also be entirely white, or albino (right).

There are hundreds of different species of catfish. The
walking catfish is among the most unusual catfish species.

It can breathe air and live without water for a while, as long as its body stays moist. It can drag and wriggle itself across land. And it can bury its body in mud to help keep moist when a pond dries up. But most of the time, it lives the life of a regular catfish.

Like all native catfish, the walking catfish has no scales. Instead, it has skin that feels smooth and slippery. Picking one up and holding onto it isn't so easy!

The back of a walking catfish is dark gray or grayish brown. The sides are greenish blue, dotted with many small, white spots. The belly is light blue, gray, or tan. A walking catfish body is shaped like a tube that narrows at the tail.

The fish's head is wide and flat. Its mouth has two large, fleshy lips. Surrounding the lips are four pairs of "whiskers" called **barbels**. They're like feelers and have many sensors on them that serve as taste buds. As a catfish

Walking catfish have four sets of "whiskers" called barbels.

moves along the bottom of a lake or pond, its barbels are always touching, tapping, and tasting.

The walking catfish has small eyes and probably poor vision. When the water is muddy, the fish cannot see food. Like nearly all catfish, it is mostly **nocturnal**, or active at night. Eyes are of little use at this time anyway. It uses its barbels to locate food.

On the top and bottom of a walking catfish's mouth are patches of many sandpaper-like teeth. When feeding on a dead fish or frog, the catfish cannot take large bites. Instead, it clamps down and shakes the animal until a mouthful breaks loose.

Like other fish, the walking catfish has **gills** to draw oxygen from the water. These body parts are on both sides of the head. The walking catfish also has small, branching structures that extend from the gills. They allow the fish to draw oxygen straight from the air.

The walking catfish has several fins. A long **dorsal** fin runs almost the length of the back. Another fin runs along

The walking catfish's dorsal fin goes down the back of its body. On the sides of its body are pectoral fins.

the fish's belly. **Pectoral** fins stick out on the sides just behind the head. At the front of each pectoral fin is a hard, stiff spine that helps the catfish walk.

Walking catfish live in freshwater lakes, swamps, ponds, ditches, rice paddies, rivers, and canals. They can also survive in somewhat salty water where a river drains into the ocean.

21st CENTURY SKILLS LIBRARY

Why do walking catfish walk? When ponds or ditches dry up, many fish die. When sluggish streams or swamps lack enough oxygen, many fish can't survive. When food runs low in a river, many fish starve. However, in similar situations, the walking catfish gets busy.

A walking catfish starts by pressing its spines into the ground. Bending from side to side, it shifts its weight back and forth between the spines. It wriggles up out of the water and begins breathing air. Then it heads off in search of a better home. Walking catfish can live out of water for up to 30 hours, as long as it is raining or there's enough water on the ground to slither through.

These catfish prefer warm areas. When the weather becomes too cold and dry, they burrow into the muddy banks or bottoms of their ponds or streams. Their breathing and heart rates slow down. Body functions come almost to a stop. Silent and buried, the fish

Large waterbirds such as the great blue heron feed on walking catfish.

remain here until warm, wet weather returns. It can

take months.

During the spring, males and females form pairs and

build nests. Together, they create a shallow pit in the

sediment. Later, the female lays a sticky mass of as many as 1,000 eggs. The eggs hatch about 30 hours later.

The parents protect the tiny **larvae** from **predators** for two or three days. Then the young walking catfish are on their own.

The fish feed on insects, other small fish, worms, crayfish, dragonflies, and plants. In turn, other fish, storks, egrets, and other large waterbirds feed on the walking catfish.

If they manage to escape these predators, most walking catfish reach a length of about 15 inches (38 centimeters). The largest ones are about 2 feet (61 cm) long.

Catfish usually have spines on their pectoral fins. The spines flare out to the sides when the fish senses danger. With the fins and spines flared, the catfish looks larger and more threatening to its enemies. It might be enough to scare away some attackers. The spines also make it harder for a predator to swallow the fish. Tall waterbirds such as egrets do manage to eat catfish, but only if they do it just right. How do you think they swallow them—head first or tail first? Why?

CHAPTER THREE

IT'S TOO FAR TO WALK

A walking catfish walks over wet grass.

Years ago, walking catfish were found only in Southeast Asia. They lived in India, Sri Lanka, Bangladesh, Thailand, Cambodia, Indonesia, Singapore, Borneo, and several other countries. These lands have been the fish's home for centuries.

Today, people catch walking catfish to feed their families. People also sell them in fish markets. Because these fish can breathe air, people can catch, transport, and sell them while they are still alive. They are the freshest fish at the market!

In recent years, the walking catfish has spread to China and Hong Kong, the Philippines, the United States, Japan, Taiwan, and other places. How did they reach these countries? Did they walk?

In fact, it was human activity that spread these fish to so many different countries. Fish farmers imported them to raise for food. Homeowners imported them to fill backyard ponds. Pet store owners brought them in to sell. As long as the walking catfish stayed where they belonged in these new countries, everything was fine. But, of course, that did not happen.

People brought walking catfish to Florida in the early 1960s. The fish soon began leaving their new homes. They

A family watches walking catfish cross a street!

21st CENTURY SKILLS LIBRARY

wriggled away from farms and made their way to ponds and ditches. They can be poor pets, so some aquarium owners released them into lakes and streams. Some homeowners with outdoor ponds discovered that their fish had abandoned them. By 1968, the walking catfish was living in the wild in three Florida counties.

Lawmakers knew that the walking catfish was spreading. They made it illegal to sell or own the fish in Florida. So, many people dumped their walking catfish into ponds, streams, lakes, and rivers. The walking catfish survived well in the wild. By 1978, they had spread to 20 Florida counties.

21st Century Content

In 1969, U.S. Fish and Wildlife Service officials banned citizens from owning walking catfish and their eggs without a special permit. They, along with the Florida Fish and Wildlife Conservation Commission, wanted to stop the spread of walking catfish in order to protect Florida's **ecosystems**. But there were also economic concerns about the walking catfish. Unchecked, walking catfish populations would harm fish farming businesses in Florida. This law now protects the fish farming industry.

Walking catfish have lived in Southeast Asia for years—perhaps even millions of years. Over such a long time, it seems that the catfish could have walked to every country on Earth. Why hasn't this happened?

Most walking catfish living in the wild in the United States live in Florida. However, they occasionally turn up in California, Connecticut, Georgia, Massachusetts, and Nevada. In these states, people probably kept the catfish originally as pets. Then, either people released them on purpose or the fish left on their own. Whatever the case, these fish survived only in Florida, where it is warm enough for them to live in the wild.

CHAPTER FOUR

THE PROBLEM WITH WALKING CATFISH

There are hundreds of catfish species in the world, including striped catfish. This is a school of young striped catfish.

Walking catfish are just one of many catfish species. And they have existed for many years. So why are people so alarmed when they move into a new country?

Walking catfish cause a number of problems. They sometimes invade fish farms. They eat tadpoles and small native fishes, especially in small ponds. And they can carry **organisms** that cause disease.

ANIMAL INVADERS: WALKING CATFISH

19

Invasive water species are a threat to most fish farms.

Farmers in many states earn their living raising fish. A single farmer can raise thousands of trout, bass, catfish, or minnows in a year. The farmer might stock a lake with these fish or sell them as bait.

Fish farming can be difficult, expensive work. The farmers must maintain ponds or tanks full of clean water at the proper temperature. They must also provide plenty of high-quality food. The fish must be free of diseases. Fish farmers work hard to keep everything just right for their fish.

Walking catfish have sometimes invaded fish farms in Florida. They hike right into those carefully maintained ponds and eat food meant for the farm fish. They also eat the fish themselves. One farmer reported walking catfish in his pond shortly after a hurricane. By the time he spotted the invaders, they had already eaten many of his valuable fish!

Walking catfish also make trouble for fish in the wild. During dry periods, lakes and ponds shrink. They can turn into muddy fields with scattered pools. Native fish, water turtles, and frogs become trapped in those small pools. Sometimes, there is just enough food and oxygen in these pools for them to survive until it rains again.

But when walking catfish move in, it is a different story. These hardy fish eat the available food from the water and then breathe air when oxygen in the water runs low. They stay while the food supply dwindles and the other animals die.

Walking catfish can also wipe out populations of tadpoles. In the spring, frogs lay thousands of eggs in pools, ditches, and ponds. The eggs hatch into tiny, swimming tadpoles—tasty, tender snacks for the walking catfish. The catfish might eat all of the tadpoles in one pond, then walk to the next pond and do it again.

CHAPTER FIVE

FISHING FOR SOLUTIONS

When an animal invades a new country, different groups of people take action. They look at all the possible ways to deal with the species. Scientists who study animals, or **zoologists**, examine how the animal behaves, what it eats, and where it lives. Airport and shipyard workers figure out how to prevent these animals from entering the country. Government officials think of ways to stop the spread of the animal. Invasive species experts research how other countries have dealt with the animal invader.

All these groups worked on ways to manage the invasion of walking catfish in the United States. Zoologists knew that cutting off their food supply was impossible, because the fish eats so many different things. They also knew that poisoning the walking catfish would endanger insects, frogs, turtles, birds, and other fish. Draining ponds

Experts recognize that poisoning walking catfish would threaten all the animals that feed on them, including this native largemouth bass.

was out of the question, too, because the catfish could just walk to other ponds.

Early on, the government passed laws against owning a walking catfish. At first, this made things worse. Some people dumped their fish into nearby ponds and streams. But since then, the law has been helpful. Airport workers now watch for travelers sneaking the fish into the United States. Pet shop owners know they cannot sell the fish in their stores.

Fish farmers have also come up with ways to keep the walking catfish out. They built mounds of dirt and wire fences around their ponds.

Fortunately, the fish cannot survive in cold weather. Even though it walks and buries itself in mud to escape tough conditions, it cannot survive very cold temperatures for long. This need for warm temperatures has kept the fish from spreading north beyond Florida. It has also kept the walking catfish from invading countries with cooler weather.

Right now, experts disagree on the dangers of the walking catfish. Some believe that it is simply blending into its new environment. They point to areas of Florida where the catfish population has dropped. And they say

Nearly everyone agrees that Florida's walking catfish population is no longer growing and has even decreased. When these fish first appeared in Florida, the story made big news. People could not read enough about the fish that walked down sidewalks and crossed highways. They called the walking catfish a monster, or "Frankenfish." Some experts believe that press coverage overstated the walking catfish danger. More than 40 years since the walking catfish first came to Florida, expert opinion still varies. Do you think people overreacted to the problem at first? Why or why not?

An egret in southern Florida holds a walking catfish in its bill.

there is no information proving the walking catfish has damaged the survival of native fishes. Others feel that the fish is one of the worst invasive species on Earth.

There will always be disagreements, but one thing is certain. The best way to deal with an invasive species is to prevent it from invading in the first place. This is an important lesson for us to learn.

The Invasive Species Specialist Group (ISSG) is an international organization of experts that works to solve invasive species problems around the world. The ISSG selects and describes the invasive species and lists the invaded countries. It also outlines methods to prevent, control, or wipe out invasive populations. Right now, no one knows exactly how many invasive species there are. The ISSG lists almost 500 species. It adds about 100 new species to its list each year. By working together to prevent the spread of animal invaders, **conservation** organizations, zoologists, lawmakers, and ordinary citizens around the world can make a difference.

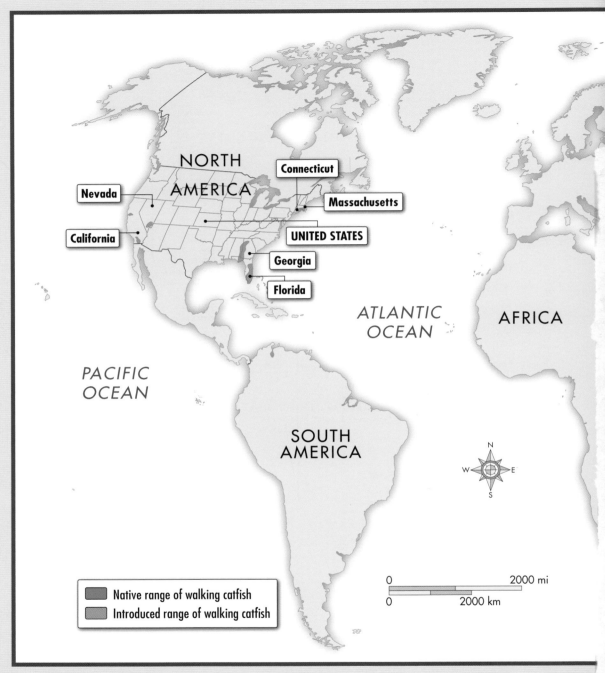

NORTH
AMERICA

Connecticut

Nevada

Massachusetts

California

UNITED STATES

Georgia

Florida

ATLANTIC
OCEAN

AFRICA

PACIFIC
OCEAN

SOUTH
AMERICA

N
W E
S

Native range of walking catfish
Introduced range of walking catfish

0   2000 mi
0   2000 km

This map shows where in the world the walking catfish

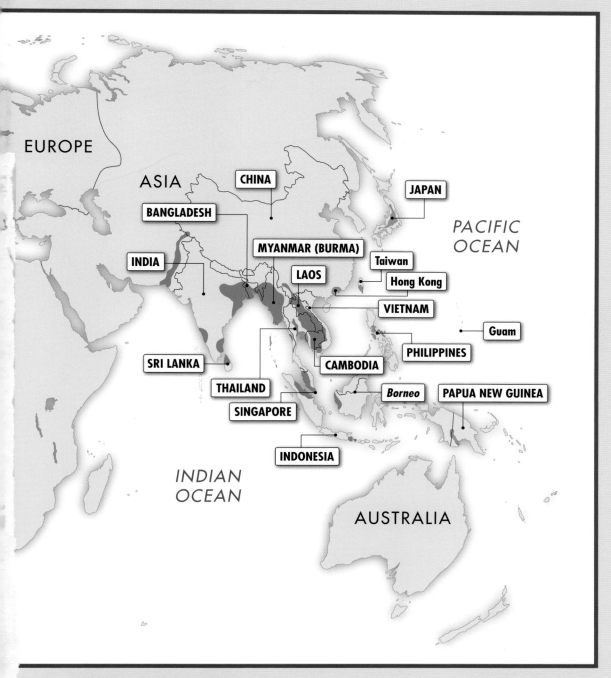

EUROPE

ASIA

CHINA

JAPAN

PACIFIC
OCEAN

BANGLADESH

MYANMAR (BURMA)

Taiwan

INDIA

LAOS

Hong Kong

VIETNAM

Guam

PHILIPPINES

SRI LANKA

CAMBODIA

THAILAND

Borneo

PAPUA NEW GUINEA

SINGAPORE

INDONESIA

INDIAN
OCEAN

AUSTRALIA

lives naturally and where it has invaded.

GLOSSARY

barbels (BAR-buhlz) whiskerlike structures around the mouth of certain fishes, such as catfish

conservation (kon-sur-VAY-shuhn) the preservation, management, and care of natural resources such as forests and wildlife

dorsal (DOR-suhl) on or near the back of an animal

ecosystems (EE-koh-siss-tuhmz) communities of plants, animals, and other organisms together with their environment, working as a unit

gills (GILZ) body parts of water animals, such as fish, used to draw oxygen from the water

larvae (LAR-vee) the very young, undeveloped forms of certain animals such as fish or insects

nocturnal (nok-TUR-nuhl) active at night

organisms (OR-guh-niz-uhmz) individual forms of life, such as plants, animals, or bacteria

pectoral (PEHK-ter-uhl) on or near the chest of an animal

predators (PRED-uh-turz) animals that hunt other animals for food

sediment (SED-ih-ment) the sand and gravel that settle on the bottom of a lake or pond

species (SPEE-sheez) a group of similar plants or animals

zoologists (zoe-AHL-uh-jists) scientists who study animals

FOR MORE INFORMATION

Books

DK Publishing. *E.encyclopedia Animal*. New York: DK Children, 2005.

Lantz, Peggy S. *The Young Naturalist's Guide to Florida*.
Sarasota, FL: Pineapple Press, 2006.

Silverstein, Virginia, Alvin Silverstein, and Laura Silverstein Nunn.
Fabulous Fish. Brookfield, CT: Twenty-First Century, 2003.

Web Sites

Florida's Exotic Freshwater Fishes—Walking Catfish
floridafisheries.com/Fishes/non-native.html#walking
For more information about walking catfish from the Florida
Fish and Wildlife Conservation Commission

Global Invasive Species Database: *Clarias batrachus*
www.issg.org/database/species/ecology.asp?si=62&fr=1&sts=sss
To find out more about this invading catfish

Science News for Kids—Alien Invasions
www.sciencenewsforkids.org/articles/20040512/Feature1.asp
For an explanation of the problems created by various invasive plant and animal species

INDEX

ABOUT THE AUTHOR

Susan H. Gray has a master's degree in zoology. She has written more than 90 science and reference books for children, and especially loves writing about animals. Gray also likes to garden and play the piano. She lives in Cabot, Arkansas, with her husband, Michael, and many pets.